Introduction to

No-Knead Pizza,

Restaurant Style Flatbread

& More

From the kitchen of
Artisan Bread with Steve

Updated 5.10.16

By
Steve Gamelin

Now that I have met the standard legal requirements I would like to give my personal exceptions. I understand this is a cookbook and anyone who purchases this book can, (a) print and share the recipes with their friends, as you do with your other cookbooks (of course, it is my hope they too will start to make no-knead bread and buy my cookbooks) and (b) you may share a recipe or two on your website, etc. as long as you note the source and provide instructions on how your audience can acquire this book.

Thanks – Steve

Table of Contents

Quick Note from Steve

You'll be pleasantly surprised with how easy it is to make pizza dough. Just mix... wait... and poof, you have pizza dough. In fact... sometimes we spend more time running around getting a pizza than it takes to make great tasting pizzas. The cost of the ingredients to make pizza dough is less than $1 and once you've made your own fresh pizza dough... you'll never go back.

What makes this cookbook unique is the technique. I use a process called "degas, pull & stretch" which replaces folding and shaping... and a process called "roll-to-coat" to dust the dough with flour in the mixing bowl. In other words... I can make pizza dough in a glass bowl with a spoon... without ever touching the dough. I call it "hands-free" because you won't touch the dough until you roll it out of the mixing bowl to shape into a pizza which is demonstrated on YouTube in World's Easiest Pizza Dough... ready to bake in less than 2 hours (no-knead "hands-free" technique).

There's more... I've included "The Perfect Little 9" Pizza" (they're fun, fast and convenient), a selection of "Restaurant Style Flatbread" recipes (have you ever wondered how restaurants make the dough for their appetizer pizzas?), and a couple other recipes you're sure to enjoy.

I hope this becomes one of your "can't do without" cookbooks.

Thanks – Steve

Two Basic Methods for Making No-Knead Bread

There are two basic methods… traditional and turbo.

"Traditional" No-Knead Bread… proof for 8 to 24 hours

The traditional no-knead method uses long proofing times (8 to 12 hours) to develop flavor and was designed to be baked in a Dutch oven. The purpose of the Dutch oven is to emulate a baker's oven by trapping the moisture from the dough in a "screaming" hot, enclosed environment. This is an excellent method for making artisan quality bread.

Recommended YouTube video: <u>World's Easiest Bread Recipe & Technique for Beginners (no kneading… using "hands-free" technique)</u> (Oct 6, 2015 – 6:52)

No-Knead "Turbo" Bread… ready to bake in 1-1/2 hours

The no-knead "Turbo" method uses shorter proofing times (ready to bake in 2-1/2 hours) and was designed to be baked in traditional bakeware (bread pan, etc.). It was designed for those who want to make no-knead bread, but… don't want to wait 8 to 24 hours. Those who want bread machine bread, but… don't want to buy and store a bread machine. It's for those of you who want a fast reliable way to make fresh from the oven bread without the hustle of expensive machines, Dutch ovens, or kneading.

Recommended YouTube video: <u>Ultimate Introduction to No-Knead "Turbo" Bread… ready to bake in 2-1/2 hours</u> (Mar 8, 2015 – 9:03 min)

Advantages of No-Knead Bread

- No kneading… Mother Nature does the kneading for you.

- No yeast proofing… instant yeast doesn't require proofing.

- No special equipment (no mixer, no bread machine) the entire process is done in a glass bowl with a spoon and a spatula… and can be baked in a wide variety of baking vessels (standard bread pan, uncovered baker, skillet, preheated Dutch oven, etc.).

- Only uses 4 basic ingredients (flour, salt, yeast and water) to which other ingredients can be added to make a variety of specialty breads.

Advantage of the Traditional Method

- If you want bread tomorrow. When I the dough is proof over night it is available at your convenience any time the next day… it fits easily into your schedule.

Advantages of "Turbo" Method

- If you want bread later today. Shorter proofing time... bread is ready to bake in less than 2-1/2 hours.

- Some have said, no-knead "Turbo" bread is bread machine bread... without the bread machine. I like to think of it as a way for the average family to have fresh-from-the-oven bread in the convenience of their homes without special equipment or any hassles.

"Turbo" Ingredients & Technique

There are two changes... ingredients and sound proofing technique.

(1) Ingredients

Yeast is the active ingredient that makes the dough rise, thus shorter proofing times require more yeast. As a result, the recipe calls for 1-1/4 teaspoons yeast.

(2) Sound proofing technique

Use a warm bowl, warm ingredients and warm proofing environment. The ideal temperature for proofing is 78 to 85 degrees F, but the typically home is 68 to 72 degrees, which is why recipes generally suggest proofing in a "warm draft-free environment". So, you have a choice... wait longer for the dough to proof or create a warm proofing environment. My favorite techniques for creating a warm proofing environment are...

Oven setting: If your oven has a setting for proofing (80 degrees F)... use it.

Direct sunlight: Cover bowl with plastic wrap, place in direct sunlight, and the heat from the Sun will create a more favorable proofing environment.

Oven light: If your oven has a light... cover bowl with plastic wrap, place in oven, turn light on, and close the door. The oven light will generate heat and increase the temperature inside the oven by several degrees. The amount of heat will depend on the size of the oven and strength of the bulb. The oven temperature will start low and climb slowly. Each oven is different, so check periodically until you are familiar with the nature of your oven.

Desk Lamp: Cover bowl with plastic wrap, place under a desk lamp, lower lamp so that it's close to the bowl, and turn lamp on. The plastic wrap over the bowl will create a similar effect to leaving car windows rolled up on a sunny day.

Supporting video: <u>How to Proof Bread Dough (a.k.a. The Dynamics of Proofing)</u>

Ingredients

It only takes four ingredients to make bread... flour, salt, yeast and water.

Flour

Flour is the base ingredient of bread and there are four basic types of flour...

(1) Bread flour is designed for yeast bread. It has a higher percentage of gluten which gives artisan bread its airy crumb.

(2) All-purpose flour has less gluten than bread flour. I use all-purpose flour for biscuits, flatbreads, etc. In other words... I use it when I don't want an airy crumb.

(3) Self-rising flour is all-purpose flour with baking soda and baking powder added as leavening agents. It's intended for quick breads... premixed and ready to go. Do not use self-rising flour to make yeast bread. To see the difference between yeast and quick breads you may want to watch Introduction to No-Knead Beer Bread (a.k.a. Artisan Yeast Beer Bread) and Introduction to Quick Beer Bread (a.k.a. Beer Bread Dinner Rolls).

(4) And there are a variety of specialty flours... whole wheat, rye, and a host of others. Each has its unique flavor and characteristics. In some cases, you can substitute specialty flour for bread flour, but you may need to tweak the recipe because most specialty flours have less gluten. I frequently blend specialty flour with bread flour.

4

Flour is the primary ingredient... if you don't use the correct flour you won't get the desired results.

Note: To know how many cups of flour there are in a specific bag... it's typically on the side in "Nutritional Facts". For example, this bag reads, "Serving Size 1/4 cup... Serving Per Container about 75". In other words... 18.75 (75 times 1/4). That's the technical answer, but in the real world (measuring cup versus weight) a bag of flour will measure differently based on density (sifted versus unsifted), type of flour (wheat is more dense than bread flour), humidity (flour weighs more on humid days), and all the other variables life and nature have to offer. Thus, there is no single correct answer, but for practical purposes... figure a 5 lb bag of bread flour is 17 to 18 cups.

Salt

While it is possible to make bread without salt... you would be disappointed. There are three basics types of salt...

(1) Most baking recipes are designed to use everyday table salt unless specified otherwise. Unless you're experienced, it is probably smartest to use table salt for your baking needs.

(2) Kosher salt is excellent. I use it when I cook, but a tablespoon of kosher salt does not equal a tablespoon of table salt because kosher salt crystals are larger.

(3) And, I use specialty salt as a garnish... for appearance and taste. For example, I use sea salt to garnish pretzels.

Generally speaking, when salt is added as an ingredient and baked it is difficult to taste the difference between table, kosher and sea salt. When salt is added as a garnish and comes in contact with the taste buds... kosher or specialty salt is an excellent choice.

Yeast

Yeast is the "magic" ingredient which transforms flour and water into dough. My traditional no-knead recipes use 1/4 tsp yeast... I want the dough to rise slowly which allows the dough to develop flavor. My "Turbo" recipes use 1-1/4 tsp yeast... I want a faster rises like traditional bread recipes. There are three basic types of yeast...

(1) The most common is active dry yeast which needs to be proof in warm water prior to being added to flour.

(2) I use instant dry yeast (a.k.a. "instant yeast", "bread machine yeast", "quick rise", "rapid rise", "fast rising", etc.) which does not need to be proofed in warm water. It is a more recent development which is more

potent and reliable... and why worry about proofing yeast if you don't have too.

(3) Some older recipes call for <u>cake yeast</u> (a.k.a. "compressed yeast" or "fresh yeast"), but it's perishable. Most bakers substitute active and instant dry yeast for cake yeast when using older recipes.

The names on the bottles can be confusing. When in doubt, read the instructions and look for one that does not require soaking the yeast in warm water prior to use.

Water

Water hydrates the ingredients and activates the yeast. The no-knead method uses a little more water than the typical recipe... and that's a good thing. It makes it easier to combine the wet and dry ingredients, and contributes to its airy crumb.

(1) I use <u>tap water</u>. It's convenient and easy, but sometimes city water has too much chlorine (chlorine kills yeast).

(2) If your dough does not rise during first proofing you may want to use <u>bottled drinking water</u>.

(3) But, do not use <u>distilled water</u> because the minerals have been removed.

Water is a flavor ingredient, if your water doesn't taste good... use bottled drinking water.

Flavor Ingredients

It only takes four ingredients to make bread... flour, salt, yeast and water, to which a variety of flavor ingredients can be added to make specialty breads such as... honey whole wheat, multi-grain white, rosemary, Mediterranean olive, cinnamon raisin, honey oatmeal, and a host of others.

Technique & Tips

The techniques used to make traditional and "Turbo" no-knead bread are identical except proofing. Turbo uses shorter proofing times, thus it is important to use sound proofing technique (a warm proofing environment) when using the "Turbo" method. The technique discussed in this section is demonstrated on YouTube in <u>World's Easiest Pizza Dough... ready to bake in less than 2 hours (no-knead "hands-free" technique)</u> ("Turbo" method) and <u>Easy No-Knead Pizza Dough (Mix... Wait... Poof, you have Pizza Dough)</u> ("traditional" method, but was filmed prior to developing "hands-free" technique).

Prep
Traditional: Because the traditional method proof for 8 to 24 hours it uses cool water to slow the proofing process, thus the temperature of the bowl is not important.

Turbo: To insure consistency and assist Mother Nature with proofing... it's important to provide yeast with a warm proofing environment. One of the keys to proofing temperature is the temperature of the mixing bowl because it has direct contact with the dough. Thus, use a bowl that is warm to the touch so that the bowl doesn't draw the heat out of the warm water.

Combining Ingredients
Pour water in a 3 to 4 qt glass mixing bowl (use warm water and a warm bowl for "Turbo" and cool for traditional). Add salt, yeast, flavor ingredients, etc... and stir to combine (it will insure the ingredients are evenly distributed). Add flour (flour will resist the water and float). Start by stirring the ingredients with the handle end of a plastic spoon drawing the flour from the sides into the middle of bowl (vigorously mixing will not hydrate the flour faster... but it will raise a lot of dust). Within 30 seconds the flour will hydrate and form a shaggy ball. Then scrape dry flour from side of bowl and tumble dough to combine moist flour with dry flour (about 15 seconds). It takes about one minute to combine wet and dry ingredients.

Traditional: Cover bowl with plastic wrap, place on counter, and proof for 8 to 24 hours.

Turbo: Cover bowl with plastic wrap, place in a warm draft free location, and proof for 1-1/2 hours.

1st Proofing (bulk fermentation)
The process is called "proofing" because it "proves" the yeast is active.

Bread making is nature at work (yeast is a living organism) and subject to nature. Seasons (summer vs. winter) and weather (heat & humidity) have a direct impact on proofing. In other words, don't worry if your dough varies in size... that's Mother Nature. Just focus on your goal... if the gluten forms (dough develops a stringy nature) and doubles in size... you're good to go.

If your dough does <u>not</u> rise the usual culprits are... outdated yeast or chlorinated water (chlorine kills yeast). Solution, get fresh yeast and/or use bottled drinking water.

If your dough is <u>slow</u> (takes "forever") to rise... your proofing temperature is probably too cool.

Traditional: Because the traditional method use long proofing times (8 to 24 hours) it does not require any special technique.

Turbo: Because "Turbo" dough use shorter proofing times (1-12/ hours) it is important to practice sound proofing technique.

The ideal temperature for proofing is 78 to 85 degrees F, but the typically home is 68 to 72 degrees, which is why recipes generally suggest proofing in a "warm draft-free environment". So, you have a choice... wait longer or create a warm proofing environment. My favorites are...

Oven setting: If your oven has a setting for proofing (80 degrees F)... use it.

Direct sunlight: Cover bowl with plastic wrap, place in direct sunlight, and the heat from the Sun will create a favorable proofing environment.

Oven light: If your oven has a light... cover bowl with plastic wrap, place in oven, turn light on, and close the door. The oven light will generate heat and increase the temperature inside the oven by several degrees. The amount of heat will depend on the size of the oven and strength of the bulb. The oven temperature will always start low and climb slowly, but it may go over 90 degrees F. so check periodically until you are familiar with the nature of your oven.

Desk Lamp: Cover bowl with plastic wrap, place under a desk lamp, lower lamp so that it's close to the bowl, and turn lamp on. The plastic wrap over the bowl will create a similar effect to leaving car windows rolled up on a sunny day.

Microwave: Place an 8 to 16 oz cup of water in the microwave and heat on high for 2 minutes. Then move the cup to the back corner, place mixing bowl (dough) in microwave and close the door. The heat and steam from the hot water will create a favorable environment for proofing.

Folding dough proofer: Commercial bakeries have large proofing ovens in which they can control climate and temperature. There are smaller versions available for the public that fold flat.

Tip: To fit bread making into your schedule... you can extend 1st proofing up to 4 hours (or even more), but don't shorten... it important to give Mother Nature time to form the gluten.

Degas, Pull & Stretch

The purpose of degassing, pulling and stretching is to, (a) expel the gases that formed during bulk fermentation, (b) strengthen the dough by realigning and stretching the gluten strands, and (c) stimulate yeast activity for 2nd proofing.

Because no-knead dough is sticky and difficult to handle... I degas, pull & stretch dough by stirring it in the bowl with the handle end of a plastic spoon (like a dough hook). It will reduce the size of the dough ball by 50% making it easier to handle and the process replaces folding and shaping in most cases.

Roll-to-Coat

Before removing the dough from bowl... dust the dough and side of the bowl with flour, then roll-to-coat. The flour will bond to the sticky dough making it easier to handle, but do not roll-to-coat with flour if you're going to garnish or baste.

Garnish & Baste

The purpose of garnishing and basting is to enhance the appearance of the crust, but it isn't necessary. If you decide to garnish and baste there are two techniques... roll-to-coat and skillet method.

Roll-to-Coat Method: Before removing dough from bowl... add ingredients to bowl (on the dough and side of the bowl), then roll to coat. For example, when I garnish honey oatmeal bread... I sprinkle oat in the bowl and on the dough, then roll the dough ball in the oats and they will bond to the sticky dough. This can also be done with seeds, grains, olive oil, egg wash, etc.

Skillet Method: When I want to garnish and/or baste the top of the loaf... I coat the proofing skillet with baste (egg wash, olive oil, vegetable oil, etc.) and sprinkle with the garnish (oats, seeds, grains, etc.). The ingredients will bond with the dough as the dough proofs.

Supporting video: <u>How to Garnish & Baste No-Knead Bread using "Hands-Free" Technique</u>

Divide & Shape

If you're not going to divide the dough... it can go straight from the mixing bowl to the proofing skillet or baking vessel. If you are going to divide and shape the dough... dust the dough and side of the bowl with flour and roll-to-coat, dust work surface with flour, roll the dough ball out of the bowl (excess flour and all) onto the work surface, and divide and shape. I use a plastic bowl scraper to assist in dividing, shaping and carry the dough to the baking vessel. Together they (flour & bowl scraper) make it easier to handle the dough.

2nd Proofing

Traditional: Originally I proofed for 1 to 2 hours, but over time I have been baking more in bread pans and found shorter proofing times gave better results. I now proof for 30 to 60 minutes.

Turbo: Place dough in a warm draft-free location and proof for 30 minutes.

Tip: To fit bread making into your schedule... you can extend 2nd proofing times, but you don't want the dough to exceed the size of the baking vessel. If you're using a large baking vessel (Dutch oven, etc.) it's never a problem, but if you're using a bread pan don't allow the dough to exceed the sides of the pan before baking or your loaf will droop over the sides and be less attractive. But, always bake it... it will still be delicious.

Score

The purpose of scoring dough is to provide seams to control where the crust will split during "oven spring", but it isn't necessary to score dough. If you do decide to score your loaf you may want to use a scissors (no-knead dough is very moist and more likely to stretch than slice). Personally, I place the dough in the baking vessel seam side up... the dough will split at the seam during "oven spring" which gives the loaf a nice rustic appearance.

Bake

Baking Time: Bread is done when it reaches an internal temperature of 185 to 220 degrees F. and the crumb (inside of the bread) isn't doughy. Baking times in my recipes are designed to give bread an internal temperature of 200 to 205 degrees F, but ovens vary and you may need to adjust your baking times slightly.

No-Stick Spray: Most bakeware has a non-stick surface, but it is safest to spray your bakeware unless you are fully confident your bread won't stick.

Ovens: Ovens aren't always accurate. I check the temperature of ovens and bakeware. Ovens with a digital readout that displays the temperature as they preheat are typically very accurate, but ovens that say they will be at temperature in a specific number of minutes are not always accurate. My point is... you will get the best results if you learn the character and nature of your oven.

Oven Rack: Generally speaking you want to bake bread and rolls in the middle or lower third of the oven, but it isn't critical. Just keep them away from the upper heating element or they may brown a little too quickly.

Oven Spring: When dough is first put into the oven it will increase in size by as much as a third in a matter of minutes because, (a) gases trapped in the dough will expand, (b) moisture will turn into steam and try to push its way out, and (c) yeast will become highly active converting sugars into gases. The steam and gases work together to create "oven spring". Once the internal temperature of the bread reaches 120 degrees F... the yeast will begin to die and the crust will harden.

Storing Bread & Dough

After allowing bread to cool... it can be wrapped in plastic wrap, or stored in a zip-lock plastic bag, or plastic bread bags (available on the web). If you wish to keep bread for a longer period of time... slice it into portions and freeze them in a zip-lock freezer bag (remove excess air). Do not store bread in the refrigerator. Bread goes stale faster in the refrigerator.

If you wish to save dough... divide it into portions, drizzle each portion with olive oil, place in zip-lock bag, remove excess air, and refrigerate for up to two days or freeze for up to two months. To thaw dough... move dough from freezer to refrigerator the day before (12 or more hours), then place on counter for 30 minutes before use to come to room temperature.

Equipment & Bakeware

Bowl for Mixing: You can use any 3 to 4 qt bowl. I use a 3-1/2 qt glass bowl because, (a) there's ample room for the dough to expand, (b) plastic wrap sticks to glass, and (c) I don't want the rim of my bowl to exceed the width of the plastic wrap.

Measuring Spoons: I'm sure you already have measuring spoons in the kitchen... they will work just fine. If you're going to buy new, I prefer oval versus round because an oval shape will fit into jars and containers more easily.

Measuring Cups: Dry measuring cups are designed to be filled to the top and leveled. Liquid measuring cups have a pour spout and are designed to be filled to the gradations on the side (neither measures weight). Because of their design and a slight difference in volume, it is best to use the appropriate measuring cup.

Note: U.S. and metric measuring cups may be used interchangeably... there is only a slight difference (±3%). More importantly, the ingredients of a recipe measured with a set (U.S. or metric) will have their volumes in the same proportion to one another.

Spoon for Combining Wet and Dry Ingredients: A spoon is an excellent tool for combining wet and dry ingredients. Surprisingly, I found the handle end of a plastic spoon worked best for me because, I didn't have a big clump on the end like some of my other mixing utensils (which makes it easier to stir and manipulate the dough). And when you think about it... mixers don't use a paddle to mix dough, they use a hook which looks a lot like the handle end of my spoon.

Silicon Baking Mat: Silicone baking mats are very useful... I use them as reusable parchment paper (they're environmentally friendly). Silicone baking mats serve two purposes... (a) as a work surface for folding and shaping (they have excellent non-stick properties), and (b) as a baking mat... specifically when the dough is difficult to move after folding and shaping. And I slide a cookie sheet under the mat before baking (it makes it easier to put the mat into and take it out of the oven).

Spatula: I use a spatula to scrape the sides of the bowl to get the last bits of flour incorporated into the dough.

Plastic Bowl Scraper: I use a plastic bowl scraper verses a metal dough scraper because it's the better multi-tasker. I use the bowl scraper to (a) fold, shape, and divide the dough, (b) assist in transporting the dough to the proofing vessel, (c) scrape excess flour off the work surface, (d) scrape excess flour out of the bowl (after all it is a bowl scraper), and (e) scrape any remaining bits in the sink towards the disposal. It's a useful multi-tasker and you can't do all those tasks with a metal cough scraper.

Timer: I'm sure you already have a timer and it will work just fine. If you're thinking about a new one... I prefer digital because they're more accurate.

Proofing Baskets & Vessels: The purpose of a proofing basket or vessel is to pre-shape the dough prior to baking (dough will spread if it isn't contained). Because no-knead dough has a tendency to stick to the lining of proofing baskets... I use common household items as proofing vessels. For example, I use an 8" skillet (with no-stick spray) to pre-shape dough when baking in a Dutch oven. It shapes the dough during proofing, and the handle makes it easy to carry the dough and put it in the hot Dutch oven safely.

You can also proof dough in the baking vessel if it doesn't have to be preheated. For example, standard loaves are typically proof and baked in the bread pan where your bread pan shapes the loaf during proofing and baking. You can use this same principle for shaping and baking rolls and buns.

Baking Vessels: Baking vessels come in a variety of sizes, shapes and materials. You can change the appearance of the loaf by sampling changing the baking vessel.

Plastic Wrap & Proofing Towel: I use plastic wrap for 1st proofing and a lint-free towel for 2nd proofing. Plastic wrap protects dough for longer proofing times and can be used to create a favorable proofing environment (solar effect).

Cooling Rack: The purpose of a cooling rack is to expose the bottom of the loaf during the cooling process.

Bread Bags: I use plastic bread bags to store bread after they have cooled. And they're great for packaging bread as gifts. I also use paper bags as gifts when the loaf is still warm and I don't want to trap the moisture in a plastic bag... it gives a nice natural appearance.

10" Flat Whisk: I use a flat whisk to combine dry ingredients with yogurt... a flat whisk will slice through yogurt forming small clump. If you use a balloon whisk a big lump will form inside the balloon.

Pastry/Pizza Roller: When you watch shows they hand shape and toss pizza dough, but I find it more practical to use a pastry/pizza roller. It is also useful when shaping flatbread and cinnamon rolls.

"I know when food is supposed to be served in a bowl with a name on it."
Fran Fine - "The Nanny"

No-Knead Pizza Dough & Pizza

You'll be pleasantly surprised with how easy it is to make pizza dough. Just mix... wait... and poof, you have pizza dough. And, once you have pizza dough you can make pizzas, calzones, breadsticks, garlic knots or anything else your little ole' heart desires.

I have two methods for making pizza dough, "Traditional"... proof for 8 to 24 hours, and "Turbo"... proof for 1-1/2 hours. I also have two sizes (standard & personal), and two variations (whole wheat and beer) giving you an excellent choice. You can use any of the dough recipes to make any of the pizzas.

"You better cut the pizza in four pieces
because I'm not hungry enough to eat six."

Yogi Berra, Baseball Hall of Fame catcher

No-Knead Pizza Dough

I experimented with a variety of herbs, spices, and pizza dough flavor packs, but I found I preferred to add flavors to the pizza toppings versus in the dough, because the flavors I want in a vegetarian pizza are different than the flavors I add to a pepperoni pizza. And I don't use sugar, but it's okay if it's your preference.

Notes: Pizza dough (like all other flatbreads) doesn't need a 2nd proofing... it can be used immediately.

If you wish to save dough... divide into portions, drizzle each portion with olive oil, place in zip-lock bag, remove excess air, and refrigerate for up to two days or freeze for up to two months. To thaw dough... move dough from freezer to refrigerator the day before (12 or more hours), then place on counter for 30 minutes before use to come to room temperature.

"Traditional" Pizza Dough... proofs for 8 to 24 hours

The "traditional" method for making no-knead bread is very popular. The same process can be used to make pizza dough. This recipe makes two large (16") pizzas.

Pour water into a 3 to 4 qt glass mixing bowl.

       12 oz cool Water

Add salt, yeast, and olive oil... give a quick stir to combine.

       1-1/2 tsp Salt

       1/4 tsp Instant Yeast

       1 Tbsp extra-virgin Olive Oil

Add flour... stir until dough forms a shaggy ball, scrape dry flour from side of bowl, then tumble dough to combine moist flour with dry flour.

       3 cups Bread Flour

Cover bowl with plastic wrap, place in a warm draft-free location, and proof for 8 to 24 hours.

8 to 24 hours later

When dough has risen and developed its gluten structure...

"Degas, pull and stretch"... stick handle end of a plastic spoon in the dough and stir (the dough will form a sticky ball). Then, scrape the side of the bowl to get the remainder of the dough into the sticky dough ball.

"Roll-to-coat"... sprinkle dough ball and side of bowl with flour and roll-to-coat (dusting dough ball with flour will make it easier to handle and shape dough).

       2 Tbsp Bread Flour

Dust work surface with flour, roll dough (and excess flour) out of bowl onto work surface.

Press lightly to flatten... divide dough into 2 portions and form each portion into a ball.

If you aren't ready to use the pizza dough balls... cover with a lint-free towel to rest.

Congratulations... you have 2 pizza dough balls.

"Turbo" Pizza Dough... proof for 1-1/2 hours

If you don't want to wait 8 to 24 hours... this is an excellent alterative. This recipe makes two large 16" pizzas.

Pour warm water in a 3 to 4 qt warm glass mixing bowl (use a warm bowl... you don't want a cold bowl to take the heat out of the warm water).

    <u>14 oz warm Water</u>

Add salt, yeast, and olive oil... give a quick stir to combine.

    <u>1-1/2 tsp Salt</u>

    <u>1-1/4 tsp Instant Yeast</u>

    <u>1 Tbsp extra-virgin Olive Oil</u>

Add flour... stir until dough forms a shaggy ball, scrape dry flour from side of bowl, then tumble dough to combine moist flour with dry flour.

    <u>3-1/2 cups Bread Flour</u>

Cover bowl with plastic wrap, place in a warm draft-free location, and proof for 1-1/2 hours.

1-1/2 hours later

When dough has risen and developed its gluten structure...

"Degas, pull and stretch"... stick handle end of a plastic spoon in the dough and stir (the dough will form a sticky ball). Then, scrape the side of the bowl to get the remainder of the dough into the sticky dough ball.

"Roll-to-coat"... sprinkle dough ball and side of bowl with flour and roll-to-coat (dusting dough ball with flour will make it easier to handle and shape dough).

    <u>2 Tbsp Bread Flour</u>

Dust work surface with flour, roll dough (and excess flour) out of bowl onto work surface.

Press lightly to flatten... divide dough into 2 portions and form each portion into a ball.

If you aren't ready to use the pizza dough balls... cover with a lint-free towel to rest.

Congratulations... you have 2 pizza dough balls.

YouTube video in support of recipe: <u>World's Easiest Pizza Dough... ready to bake in less than 2 hours (no-knead "hands-free" technique)</u>... demonstrates "Turbo" method including "hands-free" technique for making the dough.

Personal Size Pizza Dough

The personal size will give you one large 16" or two small 12" pizzas.

Pour warm water in a 2-1/2 to 3-1/2 qt warm glass mixing bowl (use a warm bowl... you don't want a cold bowl to take the heat out of the warm water).

> 8 oz warm Water

Add salt, yeast, and olive oil... give a quick stir to combine.

> 1 tsp Salt
> 1 tsp Instant Yeast
> 2 tsp extra-virgin Olive Oil

Add flour... stir until dough forms a shaggy ball, scrape dry flour from side of bowl, then tumble dough to combine moist flour with dry flour.

> 2 cups Bread Flour

Cover bowl with plastic wrap, place in a warm draft-free location, and proof for 1-1/2 hours.

1-1/2 hours later

When dough has risen and developed its gluten structure...

"Degas, pull and stretch"... stick handle end of a plastic spoon in the dough and stir (the dough will form a sticky ball). Then, scrape the side of the bowl to get the remainder of the dough into the sticky dough ball.

"Roll-to-coat"... sprinkle dough ball and side of bowl with flour and roll-to-coat (dusting dough ball with flour will make it easier to handle and shape dough).

> 2 Tbsp Bread Flour

Dust work surface with flour, roll dough (and excess flour) out of bowl onto work surface.

Press lightly to flatten... divide dough into 2 portions and form each portion into a ball.

If you aren't ready to use the pizza dough balls... cover with a lint-free towel to rest.

Congratulations... you have 2 personal pizza dough balls.

Option:

Traditional – Use 1/4 tsp instant Yeast and "Traditional Method" (proof over night)

Whole Wheat Pizza Dough

Whole wheat pizza is becoming very popular. I think you'll like it.

Pour warm water in a 3 to 4 qt warm glass mixing bowl (use a warm bowl... you don't want a cold bowl to take the heat out of the warm water).

> 14 oz warm Water

Add salt, yeast, and olive oil... give a quick stir to combine.

> 1-1/2 tsp Salt
> 1-1/4 tsp Instant Yeast
> 1 Tbsp extra-virgin Olive Oil
> 1 tsp Honey (optional)

Add flour... stir until dough forms a shaggy ball, scrape dry flour from side of bowl, then tumble dough to combine moist flour with dry flour.

> 2 cups Bread Flour
> 1-1/2 cups Whole Wheat Flour

Cover bowl with plastic wrap, place in a warm draft-free location, and proof for 1-1/2 hours.

1-1/2 hours later

When dough has risen and developed its gluten structure...

"Degas, pull and stretch"... stick handle end of a plastic spoon in the dough and stir (the dough will form a sticky ball). Then, scrape the side of the bowl to get the remainder of the dough into the sticky dough ball.

"Roll-to-coat"... sprinkle dough ball and side of bowl with flour and roll-to-coat (dusting dough ball with flour will make it easier to handle and shape dough).

> 2 Tbsp Bread Flour

Dust work surface with flour, roll dough (and excess flour) out of bowl onto work surface.

Press lightly to flatten... divide dough into 2 portions and form each portion into a ball.

If you aren't ready to use the pizza dough balls... cover with a lint-free towel to rest.

Congratulations... you have 2 whole wheat pizza dough balls.

Options:

100% Whole Wheat – 14 oz Water | 1-1/2 tsp Salt | 1-1/4 tsp Instant Yeast | 1 Tbsp Olive Oil | 3-1/2 cups Whole Wheat Flour

Traditional – Use 1/4 tsp instant Yeast and "Traditional Method" (proof over night)

Beer Pizza Dough

One simple recipe with hundreds of options... change the wet ingredient—the beer—from a lager, to an amber, or a hefeweizen you can have a new and uniquely flavored pizza crust. It's fun to experiment with beer bread... the beer isle is full of ideas.

Gently pour beer into a 3 to 4 qt room-temperature glass mixing bowl to limit foaming.

> 14 oz room-temperature Beer

Add salt, yeast, and olive oil... give a quick stir to combine.

> 1-1/2 tsp Salt
> 1-1/4 tsp Instant Yeast
> 1 Tbsp extra-virgin Olive Oil

Add flour... stir until dough forms a shaggy ball, scrape dry flour from side of bowl, then tumble dough to combine moist flour with dry flour.

> 3-1/2 cups Bread Flour

Cover bowl with plastic wrap, place in a warm draft-free location, and proof for 1-1/2 hours.

1-1/2 hours later

When dough has risen and developed its gluten structure...

"Degas, pull and stretch"... stick handle end of a plastic spoon in the dough and stir (the dough will form a sticky ball). Then, scrape the side of the bowl to get the remainder of the dough into the sticky dough ball.

"Roll-to-coat"... sprinkle dough ball and side of bowl with flour and roll-to-coat (dusting dough ball with flour will make it easier to handle and shape dough).

> 2 Tbsp Bread Flour

Dust work surface with flour, roll dough (and excess flour) out of bowl onto work surface.

Press lightly to flatten... divide dough into 2 portions and form each portion into a ball.

If you aren't ready to use the pizza dough balls... cover with a lint-free towel to rest.

Congratulations... you have two beer flavored pizza dough balls.

Option:

Traditional – Use 1/4 tsp instant Yeast and "Traditional Method" (proof over night)

Mushroom-Black Olive Pizza

Prep: Move rack to the middle of oven and preheat to 450 degrees F.

Shape: Place dough in the center of work space, press firmly to flatten... then work from the center pushing the dough outward to make a larger disk adding flour as needed.

 1 Pizza Dough Ball

Pick disk up by the edge and move your hands along the edge allowing gravity to stretch the dough until it forms a larger circle... then use a pizza roller to finish shaping and place in pizza pan.

Toppings: Spread a thin layer of sauce on the dough, generously sprinkle with cheese, cover with mushrooms, add black olives, and sprinkle with a little more cheese.

 3 heaping Tbsp Pizza Sauce
 8 oz shredded Provolone-Mozzarella Cheese
 6 oz sliced Mushrooms
 1/2 cup (2-1/4 oz can) sliced Black Olives

Bake: Put pan in oven and bake for 15 to 18 minutes depending on the thickness of the crust, the toppings, and how you like your cheese.

Serve: Remove from oven, slice and serve.

Pepperoni Pizza

Prep: Move rack to the middle of oven and preheat to 450 degrees F.

Shape: Place dough in the center of work space, press firmly to flatten... then work from the center pushing the dough outward to make a larger disk adding flour as needed.

  1 Pizza Dough Ball

Pick disk up by the edge and move your hands along the edge allowing gravity to stretch the dough until it forms a larger circle... then use a pizza roller to finish shaping and place in pizza pan.

Toppings: Spread a thin layer of sauce on dough, generously sprinkle with cheese, and cover with pepperoni (I didn't add a second layer of cheese because pepperoni pizza looks better if you don't cover the meat).

  3 heaping Tbsp Pizza Sauce
  8 oz shredded Provolone-Mozzarella Cheese
  Sliced Pepperoni

Bake: Put pan in oven and bake for 15 to 18 minutes depending on the thickness of the crust, the toppings, and how you like your cheese.

Serve: Remove from oven, slice and serve.

Whole Wheat Cheese Pizza

Prep: Move rack to the middle of oven and preheat to 450 degrees F.

Shape: Place dough in the center of work space, press firmly to flatten... then work from the center pushing the dough outward to make a larger disk adding flour as needed.

<u>1 Whole Wheat Pizza Dough Ball</u>

Pick disk up by the edge and move your hands along the edge allowing gravity to stretch the dough until it forms a larger circle... then use a pizza roller to finish shaping and place in pizza pan.

Toppings: Spread a thin layer of sauce on dough and generously cover with cheese.

<u>3 heaping Tbsp Pizza Sauce</u>
<u>10 oz shredded Provolone-Mozzarella Cheese</u>
<u>2 oz shredded Cheddar Cheese</u>

Bake: Put pan in oven and bake for 15 to 18 minutes depending on the thickness of the crust, the toppings, and how you like your cheese.

Serve: Remove from oven, slice and serve.

Meatball & Bacon Pizza

Prep: Move rack to the middle of oven and preheat to 450 degrees F.

Meatballs... place meatballs on a paper plate, microwave on high for 1 minute, cut in half and set aside.

<u>12 sm frozen Meatballs</u>

Bacon... trim off excess fat (not all), put paper towel on a paper plate, place bacon in a single layer on one side of the paper towel, fold other side over to cover (prevents splattering), and heat in the microwave on high for 1 to 2 minutes to render the fat, but don't overcook... it's going to be baked.

<u>4 slices Bacon</u>

Take bacon out of the microwave, remove paper towel, and allow bacon to cool... then cut bacon into pieces and set aside.

Shape: Place dough in the center of work space, press firmly to flatten... then work from the center pushing the dough outward to make a larger disk adding flour as needed.

<u>1 Pizza Dough Ball</u>

Pick disk up by the edge and move your hands along the edge allowing gravity to stretch the dough until it forms a larger circle... then use a pizza roller to finish shaping and place in pizza pan.

Toppings: Spread a thin layer of sauce on dough, generously sprinkle with cheese, and add bacon and meatballs.

<u>3 heaping Tbsp Pizza Sauce</u>

<u>8 oz shredded Provolone-Mozzarella Cheese</u>

Bake: Put pan in oven and bake for 15 to 18 minutes depending on the thickness of the crust, the toppings, and how you like your cheese.

Serve: Remove from oven, slice and serve.

Note: All meat should be precooked before being added to a pizza.

Garlic Breadsticks & Nuggets
Prep: Move rack to the middle of oven and preheat to 450 degrees F.
Shape: Place a silicone baking mat on the work surface and place dough in center of mat.

    1 Pizza Dough Ball

Then press lightly to flatten, drizzle with olive oil, and use a pizza roller to spread the oil and form a small circle, turn dough over, drizzle 2nd side with oil, and use roller (or rolling pin) to shape the dough into a 9" x 12" rectangle 1/4" thick.

    1 tsp extra-virgin Olive Oil per side

Toppings: Add a dab of garlic paste and spread with kitchen knife.

    2 tsp Garlic Paste

Generously brush with melted butter.

    2 Tbsp melted Butter

Sprinkle with cheese.

    Shredded Parmesan Cheese

Use a pizza cutter to cut dough into sticks. Then cut the irregular ends and edges into nuggets.
Bake: Slide cookie sheet under silicone baking mat, place dough (cookie sheet and all) into the oven and bake for 12 to 15 minutes depending on how you like your cheese.
Serve: Remove from oven, slice and serve.

Great Galloping Garlic Knots

Prep: Spray an 18" x 13" rimmed baking pan with no-stick spray... and set aside. Combine butter, garlic, herbs and cheese... and set aside.

> 4 Tbsp melted Butter
> 1 heaping tsp Minced Garlic
> 1 tsp Thyme
> 1 tsp Oregano
> 1 tsp grated Parmesan Cheese

Shape: Place dough in the center of work space, press firmly to flatten... then use a pizza roller to shape into a rectangle 12" to 14" wide and 6" to 8" high.

> 1 Pizza Dough Ball

Use a pizza cutter to cut dough into 1" wide strips 6" to 8" long.

Loosely tie strips into knots and place in rimmed baking pan.

Use a measuring spoon (1/4 tsp) to distribute garlic-butter mixture over garlic knots.

Proof: Cover with lint-free towel and proof for 30 minutes.

Prep: Move rack to the middle of oven and preheat to 400 degrees F.

Bake: Slide pan into oven and bake for 20 minutes.

Garnish & Serve: Remove garlic knots from oven, warm garlic-butter mixture in microwave, brush garlic knots with mixture and serve warm.

Notes: I like to add 1 heaping teaspoon minced garlic to the dough when making garlic knots.

Prefect Little 9" No-Knead Pizza

The Perfect Little 9" Pizza was designed to be baked in a toaster oven, but it can also be baked in a conventional oven. It's ideal for individual servings or as an appetizer.

Conventional vs. Toaster Oven

When I bake "Perfect Little 9" Pizzas" in the regular oven, I preheat the oven and bake them at 450 degrees F for 12 to 15 minutes, but my toaster oven heats faster and bakes hotter so I bake them at 400 degrees for 8 to 10 minutes (it isn't necessary to preheat a toaster oven).

Recipes are written to be baked in a conventional oven, but the process, bakeware, and size of the pizza were written and designed for a toaster oven because toaster ovens come in a variety of sizes... and you may need to slightly adapt the baking time and temperature to your toaster oven.

Saving Dough

If you wish to save dough... divide into portions, drizzle each portion with olive oil, place in zip-lock bag, remove excess air, and refrigerate for up to two days or freeze for up to two months. To thaw dough... move dough from freezer to refrigerator the day before (12 or more hours), then place on counter for 30 minutes before use to come to room temperature.

YouTube video in support of recipe: How to Make Homemade Perfect Little 9" Pizza in a Toaster Oven (No-Knead "Turbo" Pizza Dough)

Small Batch "Turbo" Pizza Dough

Pour warm water in a 2-1/2 to 3-1/2 qt warm glass mixing bowl (use a warm bowl... you don't want a cold bowl to take the heat out of the warm water).

<u>6 oz warm Water</u>

Add salt, yeast, and olive oil... give a quick stir to combine.

<u>1 tsp Salt</u>

<u>1 tsp Instant Yeast</u>

<u>2 tsp extra-virgin Olive Oil</u>

Add flour... stir until dough forms a shaggy ball, scrape dry flour from side of bowl, then tumble dough to combine moist flour with dry flour.

<u>1-1/2 cups Bread Flour</u>

Cover bowl with plastic wrap, place in a warm draft-free location, and proof for 1-1/2 hours.

1-1/2 hours later

When dough has risen and developed its gluten structure...

"Degas, pull and stretch"... stick handle end of a plastic spoon in the dough and stir (the dough will form a sticky ball). Then, scrape the side of the bowl to get the remainder of the dough into the sticky dough ball.

"Roll-to-coat"... sprinkle dough ball and side of bowl with flour and roll-to-coat (dusting dough ball with flour will make it easier to handle and shape dough).

<u>2 Tbsp Bread Flour</u>

Dust work surface with flour, roll dough (and excess flour) out of bowl onto work surface.

Press lightly to flatten... divide dough into 2 portions and form each portion into a ball.

If you aren't ready to use the pizza dough balls... cover with a lint-free towel to rest.

Options:

<u>Mix & Match</u> – You can use small batch pizza dough balls for either 12" pizzas or Perfect Little 9" Pizzas. My wife and I frequently make one of each.

<u>Traditional Method</u> – Decrease yeast from 1 tsp to 1/4 tsp and proof over night.

Large Batch "Turbo" Pizza Dough

Pour warm water in a 2-1/2 to 3-1/2 qt warm glass mixing bowl (use a warm bowl... you don't want a cold bowl to take the heat out of the warm water).

> 14 oz warm Water

Add salt, yeast, and olive oil... give a quick stir to combine.

> 1-1/2 tsp Salt
> 1-1/2 tsp Instant Yeast
> 1 Tbsp extra-virgin Olive Oil

Add flour... stir until dough forms a shaggy ball, scrape dry flour from side of bowl, then tumble dough to combine moist flour with dry flour.

> 3-1/2 cups Bread Flour

Cover bowl with plastic wrap, place in a warm draft-free location, and proof for 1-1/2 hours.

1-1/2 hours later

When dough has risen and developed its gluten structure...

"Degas, pull and stretch"... stick handle end of a plastic spoon in the dough and stir (the dough will form a sticky ball). Then, scrape the side of the bowl to get the remainder of the dough into the sticky dough ball.

"Roll-to-coat"... sprinkle dough ball and side of bowl with flour and roll-to-coat (dusting dough ball with flour will make it easier to handle and shape dough).

> 2 Tbsp Bread Flour

Dust work surface with flour, roll dough (and excess flour) out of bowl onto work surface.

Press lightly to flatten... divide dough into 2 portions and form each portion into a ball.

If you aren't ready to use the pizza dough balls... cover with a lint-free towel to rest.

Options:

Mix & Match – You can use small batch pizza dough balls for either 12" pizzas or Perfect Little 9" Pizzas. My wife and I frequently make one of each.

Traditional Method – Decrease yeast from 1 tsp to 1/4 tsp and proof over night.

Small Batch "Turbo" Whole Wheat Pizza Dough

Pour warm water in a 2-1/2 to 3-1/2 qt warm glass mixing bowl (use a warm bowl... you don't want a cold bowl to take the heat out of the warm water).

> 6 oz warm Water

Add salt, yeast, and olive oil... give a quick stir to combine.

> 1 tsp Salt
> 1 tsp Instant Yeast
> 2 tsp extra-virgin Olive Oil
> 1 tsp Honey (option)

Add flour... stir until dough forms a shaggy ball, scrape dry flour from side of bowl, then tumble dough to combine moist flour with dry flour.

> 3/4 cup Bread Flour
> 3/4 cup Whole Wheat Flour

Cover bowl with plastic wrap, place in a warm draft-free location, and proof for 1-1/2 hours.

1-1/2 hours later

When dough has risen and developed its gluten structure...

"Degas, pull and stretch"... stick handle end of a plastic spoon in the dough and stir (the dough will form a sticky ball). Then, scrape the side of the bowl to get the remainder of the dough into the sticky dough ball.

"Roll-to-coat"... sprinkle dough ball and side of bowl with flour and roll-to-coat (dusting dough ball with flour will make it easier to handle and shape dough).

> 2 Tbsp Bread Flour

Dust work surface with flour, roll dough (and excess flour) out of bowl onto work surface.

Press lightly to flatten... divide dough into 2 portions and form each portion into a ball.

If you aren't ready to use the pizza dough balls... cover with a lint-free towel to rest.

Options:

100% Whole Wheat – You can use 1-1/2 cups Whole Wheat Flour.

Mix & Match – You can use small batch pizza dough balls for either 12" pizzas or Perfect Little 9" Pizzas. My wife and I frequently make one of each.

Traditional Method – Decrease yeast from 1 tsp to 1/4 tsp and proof over night.

Perfect Little 9" Pepperoni Pizza

Prep: Move rack to the middle of oven and preheat to 450 degrees F, drizzle 9" pie pan with olive oil and set aside.

  1 tsp extra-virgin Olive Oil

Shape: Generously dust work surface with flour, place dough ball on work space and roll in flour to coat... then press firmly with the palm of your hand to flatten, use pizza roller to shape into a 9" circle and place in pan.

  1 small batch pizza Dough Ball

Finish shaping by pressing dough to cover bottom of pan.

Toppings: Spread a thin layer of sauce (too much sauce will make your crust soggy) on dough, generously sprinkle with cheese, and add pepperoni to cover.

  1 heaping Tbsp Pizza Sauce

  4 oz shredded Provolone-Mozzarella Cheese

  Pepperoni slices

Bake: Put pizza in oven and bake for 12 to 15 minutes depending on the thickness of the crust, the toppings, and how you like your cheese (I like it when the cheese just starts to turn dark brown).

Serve: Remove from oven, slice and serve.

Perfect Little 9" Cheese Pizza

Prep: Move rack to the middle of oven and preheat to 450 degrees F, drizzle 9" pie pan with olive oil and set aside.

> 1 tsp extra-virgin Olive Oil

Shape: Generously dust work surface with flour, place dough ball on work space and roll in flour to coat... then press firmly with the palm of your hand to flatten, use pizza roller to shape into a 9" circle and place in pan.

> 1 small batch pizza Dough Ball

Finish shaping by pressing dough to cover bottom of pan.

Toppings: Spread a thin layer of sauce on dough and generously cover with cheese.

> 1 heaping Tbsp Pizza Sauce
> 4 oz shredded Provolone-Mozzarella Cheese

Bake: Put pizza in oven and bake for 12 to 15 minutes depending on the thickness of the crust, the toppings, and how you like your cheese.

Serve: Remove from oven, slice and serve.

Perfect Little 9" Meatball Pizza

Prep: Move rack to the middle of oven and preheat to 450 degrees F, drizzle 9" pie pan with olive oil and set aside.

     1 tsp extra-virgin Olive Oil

Meatballs… place meatballs on a paper plate, microwave on high for 1 minute, cut in half and set aside.

     6 sm frozen Meatballs

Shape: Generously dust work surface with flour, place dough ball on work space and roll in flour to coat… then press firmly with the palm of your hand to flatten, use pizza roller to shape into a 9" circle and place in pan.

     1 small batch pizza Dough Ball

Finish shaping by pressing dough to cover bottom of pan.

Toppings: Spread a thin layer of sauce on dough, generously sprinkle with cheese, add meatballs, and sprinkle with a little more cheese.

     1 heaping Tbsp Pizza Sauce
     4 oz shredded Provolone-Mozzarella Cheese

Bake: Put pizza in oven and bake for 12 to 15 minutes depending on the thickness of the crust, the toppings, and how you like your cheese.

Serve: Remove from oven, slice and serve.

Perfect Little 9" Mushroom-Black Olive Pizza

Prep: Move rack to the middle of oven and preheat to 450 degrees F, drizzle 9" pie pan with olive oil and set aside.

>1 tsp extra-virgin Olive Oil

Shape: Generously dust work surface with flour, place dough ball on work space and roll in flour to coat... then press firmly with the palm of your hand to flatten, use pizza roller to shape into a 9" circle and place in pan.

>1 small batch pizza Dough Ball

Finish shaping by pressing dough to cover bottom of pan.

Toppings: Spread a thin layer of sauce on dough, generously sprinkle with cheese, add mushrooms to cover, add black olives, and sprinkle with a little more cheese.

>1 heaping Tbsp Pizza Sauce
>4 oz shredded Provolone-Mozzarella Cheese
>Mushrooms
>Sliced Black Olives

Bake: Put pizza in oven and bake for 12 to 15 minutes depending on the thickness of the crust, the toppings, and how you like your cheese.

Serve: Remove from oven, slice and serve.

Perfect Little 9" Veggie Pizza

Prep: Move rack to the middle of oven and preheat to 450 degrees F, drizzle 9" pie pan with olive oil and set aside.

 1 tsp extra-virgin Olive Oil

Shape: Generously dust work surface with flour, place dough ball on work space and roll in flour to coat... then press firmly with the palm of your hand to flatten, use pizza roller to shape into a 9" circle and place in pan.

 1 small batch pizza Dough Ball

Finish shaping by pressing dough to cover bottom of pan.

Toppings: Spread a thin layer of sauce on dough, generously sprinkle with cheese, add vegetables, black olives, and tomato slices, and sprinkle with a little more cheese.

 1 heaping Tbsp Pizza Sauce
 3 oz shredded Provolone-Mozzarella Cheese
 Vegetable Stir-Fry (prepackaged mix of vegetables)
 3 slices Roma Tomato

Bake: Put pizza in oven and bake for 12 to 15 minutes depending on the thickness of the crust, the toppings, and how you like your cheese.

Serve: Remove from oven, slice and serve.

Perfect Little 9" Bacon, Bacon, Bacon Pizza

Prep: Move rack to the middle of oven and preheat to 450 degrees F, drizzle 9" pie pan with olive oil and set aside.

>   1 tsp extra-virgin Olive Oil

Canadian bacon... cut into quarters and strips... and set aside.

>   2 slices Canadian Bacon

Pre-cooked bacon... cut into 1/2" sections... and set aside.

>   2 strips pre-cooked Bacon

Shape: Generously dust work surface with flour, place dough ball on work space and roll in flour to coat... then press firmly with the palm of your hand to flatten, use pizza roller to shape into a 9" circle and place in pan.

>   1 small batch pizza Dough Ball

Finish shaping by pressing dough to cover bottom of pan.

Toppings: Spread a thin layer of sauce on dough, generously sprinkle with cheese, cover with Canadian and precooked bacon, then sprinkle with bacon bits and a little more cheese.

>   1 heaping Tbsp Pizza Sauce
>   4 oz shredded Provolone-Mozzarella Cheese
>   2 tsp real Bacon Bits

Bake: Put pizza in oven and bake for 12 to 15 minutes depending on the thickness of the crust, the toppings, and how you like your cheese.

Serve: Remove from oven, slice and serve.

Perfect Little 9" Mexican Jalapeño-Chili Fiesta Pizza

Prep: Move rack to the middle of oven and preheat to 450 degrees F, drizzle 9" pie pan with olive oil and set aside.

    1 tsp extra-virgin Olive Oil

Shape: Generously dust work surface with flour, place dough ball on work space and roll in flour to coat... then press firmly with the palm of your hand to flatten, use pizza roller to shape into a 9" circle and place in pan.

    1 small batch pizza Dough Ball

Finish shaping by pressing dough to cover bottom of pan.

Toppings: Sprinkle with cheese, add chilies, peppers, and corn.

    4 oz shredded Pepper Jack or Provolone-Mozzarella Cheese
    1 whole Green Chilies (sliced lengthwise)
    12 to 16 fresh Jalapeño Peppers slices
    1/4 cup Golden Sweet Corn

Bake: Put pizza in oven and bake for 12 to 15 minutes depending on the thickness of the crust, the toppings, and how you like your cheese.

Serve: Remove from oven, slice and serve.

Perfect Little 9" Cinnamon-Sugar Pizza

Prep: Move rack to the middle of oven and preheat to 450 degrees F, drizzle 9" pie pan with olive oil and set aside.

> 1 tsp extra-virgin Olive Oil

Cinnamon-sugar mixture: Put sugar in bowl, add cinnamon, stir to combine, and set aside.

> 1 Tbsp White Sugar
> 1/2 tsp Cinnamon

Icing: Put powder sugar in medium size bowl, add 2 Tbsp milk, and use a small spatula to combine.

> 2 cups Powder Sugar
> 3 to 4 Tbsp Whole Milk

Stir until glaze begins to come together, then add 1 more Tbsp milk and continue to stir (it should be close to the correct consistency).

Continue adding milk in very small portions until glaze is thin enough to spread, but not runny. (If the glaze sits a little too long and thickens... add a little more milk and stir to thin.)

Shape: Generously dust work surface with flour, place dough ball on work space and roll in flour to coat... then press firmly with the palm of your hand to flatten, use pizza roller to shape into a 9" circle and place in pan.

> 1 small batch pizza Dough Ball

Finish shaping by pressing dough to cover bottom of pan.

Toppings: Brush dough with butter and generously sprinkle with cinnamon-sugar mixture.

> 1 Tbsp melted Butter

Bake: Put pizza in oven and bake for 12 minutes.

Serve: Remove from oven, slice, drizzle with icing, and serve.

12" Pizza

You can also shape the Perfect Little 9" Pizza into a 12" pizza.

Prep: Move rack to the middle of oven and preheat to 450 degrees F, drizzle 9" pie pan with olive oil and set aside.

    <u>1 tsp extra-virgin Olive Oil</u>

Shape: Generously dust work surface with flour, place dough ball on work space and roll in flour to coat… then press firmly with the palm of your hand to flatten, use pizza roller to shape into a 12" circle and place on a 12' pizza pan.

    <u>1 small batch pizza Dough Ball</u>

Finish shaping by pressing dough to cover pan.

Toppings: Increase the toppings 50% using any of the previous recipes.

Bake: Put pizza in oven and bake for 12 to 15 minutes depending on the thickness of the crust, the toppings, and how you like your cheese.

Serve: Remove from oven, slice and serve.

No-Knead Mediterranean Olive Focaccia

Typically ingredients are added to the top of a focaccia, but I would like to show you how I use Mediterranean olive dough to make focaccia... I think it's special... see what you think.

"Traditional" No-Knead Mediterranean Olive Dough

Prepare flavor ingredients... place sliced black olives in small bowl, slice green and kalamata olives in half and place in bowl, zest lemon over bowl and set bowl aside.

> 1/2 cup (2-1/4 oz can) sliced Black Olives
> 1/2 cup stuffed Green Olives
> 1/2 cup pitted Kalamata Olives
> Zest of 1 Lemon

Pour water in a 3 to 4 qt glass mixing bowl.

> 12 oz cool Water

Add salt, yeast, thyme, and olive oil... give a quick stir to combine.

> 1-1/2 tsp Salt
> 1/4 tsp Instant Yeast
> 1 tsp dried Thyme
> 1 Tbsp extra-virgin Olive Oil

Add flour... stir until dough forms a shaggy ball, scrape dry flour from side of bowl, then tumble dough to combine moist flour with dry flour.

> 3 cups Bread Flour

Cover bowl with plastic wrap, place in a warm draft-free location, and proof for 8 to 24 hours.

8 to 24 hours later

When dough has risen and developed its gluten structure...

"Degas, pull and stretch"... stick handle end of a plastic spoon in the dough and stir (the dough will form a sticky ball). Then, scrape the side of the bowl to get the remainder of the dough into the sticky dough ball.

"Roll-to-coat"... sprinkle dough ball and side of bowl with flour and roll-to-coat (dusting dough ball with flour will make it easier to handle and shape dough).

> 2 Tbsp Bread Flour

Dust work surface with flour, roll dough (and excess flour) out of bowl onto work surface and form into a ball.

You have a Mediterranean olive dough ball... you can now make Mediterranean olive focaccia.

No-Knead "Turbo" Mediterranean Olive Dough

Prepare flavor ingredients... place sliced black olives in small bowl, slice green and kalamata olives in half and place in bowl, zest lemon over bowl and set bowl aside.

> 1/2 cup (2-1/4 oz can) sliced Black Olives
> 1/2 cup stuffed Green Olives
> 1/2 cup pitted Kalamata Olives
> Zest of 1 Lemon

Pour warm water in a 3 to 4 qt warm glass mixing bowl (use a warm bowl... you don't want a cold bowl to take the heat out of the warm water).

> 12 oz warm Water

Add salt, yeast, thyme, and olive oil... give a quick stir to combine.

> 1-1/2 tsp Salt
> 1-1/4 tsp Instant Yeast
> 1 tsp dried Thyme
> 1 Tbsp extra-virgin Olive Oil

Add flour... stir until dough forms a shaggy ball, scrape dry flour from side of bowl, then tumble dough to combine moist flour with dry flour.

> 3-1/2 cups Bread Flour

Place bowl in a warm draft-free location, cover with a lint-free towel (or plastic wrap), and proof for 1-1/2 hours.

1-1/2 hours later

When dough has risen and developed its gluten structure...

"Degas, pull and stretch"... stick handle end of a plastic spoon in the dough and stir (the dough will form a sticky ball). Then, scrape the side of the bowl to get the remainder of the dough into the sticky dough ball.

"Roll-to-coat"... sprinkle dough ball and side of bowl with flour and roll-to-coat (dusting dough ball with flour will make it easier to handle and shape dough).

> 2 Tbsp Bread Flour

Dust work surface with flour, roll dough (and excess flour) out of bowl onto work surface and form into a ball.

You have a Mediterranean olive dough ball... you can now make Mediterranean olive focaccia.

Mediterranean Olive Focaccia

Focaccia is a thick flatbread… typically with dimples designed to hold a generous dose of olive oil and topped with olives, rosemary, and other Mediterranean flavors, but I prefer to load the dough with the ingredients. This is an absolutely delicious flatbread that is loaded with flavor.

Shape: Place 18" x 13" rimmed baking pan on work space and line with parchment paper. Roll dough out of mixing bowl into pan, press to flatten and spread. Drizzle top with olive oil and use your hands (or pizza roller) to continue to flatten and spread into a larger rectangle.

    1 Mediterranean Olive Dough Ball
    2 Tbsp extra-virgin Olive Oil

Cover with a lint-free towel and proof for 30 minutes.

30 minutes later…

Prep: Move rack to middle of oven and preheat to 400 degrees F.
Final shaping: Press dough to flatten and spread, dimple top with finger tips to create pockets and drizzle with olive oil.

    2 Tbsp extra-virgin Olive Oil

Bake: When oven has come to temperature… place pan in oven and bake for 30 minutes.
Serve: Remove from oven and serve with olive oil for dipping.

Perfect Little 9" Mediterranean Olive Focaccia

Prep: Drizzle four 9" pie pan with olive oil and set aside.

<u>1 tsp extra-virgin Olive Oil per pan</u>

Divide & pre-shape: Generously dust work surface with flour and roll dough out of mixing bowl onto work surface.

Lightly press to flatten, divide into 4 portions and set 3 aside.

<u>1 Mediterranean Olive Dough Ball</u>

Then (one portion at a time)... press firmly with the palm of your hand to flatten, use pizza roller to shape into a circle and place in pan.

Press dough to flatten and shape to cover bottom of pan (it will cover about 75% of pan).

Cover with a lint-free towel and proof for 30 minutes.

30 minutes latter...

Prep: Move rack to middle of oven and preheat to 450 degrees F,

Finish: Press dough to flatten and cover bottom of pan, dimple top with your finger tips to create pockets and drizzle with olive oil.

<u>1 Tbsp extra-virgin Olive Oil per pizza</u>

Bake: When oven has come to temperature... place pans in oven and bake for 15 minutes.

Serve: Remove from oven and serve with olive oil for dipping.

No-Knead Fougasse

Fougasse (foo/gahss) is lattice or leaf shaped bread from Provence (pro/vance), a maritime region of southeastern France bordering Italy. And, if you like nibbling on fresh from the oven bread... you'll love fougasse. Its presentation is exceptional... sure to please your family and friends.

"Traditional" No-Knead Fougasse Dough... proof for 8 to 24 hours

Pour water in a 2-1/2 to 3 qt glass mixing bowl.

> 8 oz cool Water

Add salt, yeast, herbs, and olive oil... give a quick stir to combine.

> 1 tsp Salt
> 1/4 tsp Instant Yeast
> 1 rounded tsp dried Herbes de Provence or other blend of herbs
> 1 tsp extra-virgin Olive Oil

Add flavor ingredient (optional)... give a quick stir to combine.

> 1/2 cup (2-1/4 oz can) sliced Black Olives or 1/2 heaping tsp minced Garlic (jar) or other flavor ingredient of your choice

Add flour... stir until dough forms a shaggy ball, scrape dry flour from side of bowl, then tumble dough to combine moist flour with dry flour.

> 2 cups Bread Flour

Cover bowl with plastic wrap, place in a warm draft-free location, and proof for 8 to 24 hours.

8 to 24 hours later

When dough has risen and developed its gluten structure...

"Degas, pull and stretch"... stick handle end of a plastic spoon in the dough and stir (the dough will form a sticky ball). Then, scrape the side of the bowl to get the remainder of the dough into the sticky dough ball.

"Roll-to-coat"... sprinkle dough ball and side of bowl with flour and roll-to-coat (dusting dough ball with flour will make it easier to handle and shape dough).

> 2 Tbsp Bread Flour

Place a silicone baking mat on the work surface and roll dough (and excess flour) out of bowl onto mat.

Press lightly to flatten and shape into a medium size circle... cover with a lint-free towel, and rest for 10 minutes.

Congratulations, you have a fougasse dough ball.

YouTube video in support of recipe: Easy Homemade Fougasse (no knead... no mixer... it's as easy as making pizza) demonstrates "traditional" method including "hands-free" technique for making the dough.

No-Knead "Turbo" Fougasse Dough... proof for 1-1/2 hours

Pour warm water in a 2-1/2 to 3 qt warm glass mixing bowl (use a warm bowl... you don't want a cold bowl to take the heat out of the warm water).

> 8 oz warm Water

Add salt, yeast, herbs, and olive oil... give a quick stir to combine.

> 1 tsp Salt
> 1 tsp Instant Yeast
> 1 rounded tsp dried Herbes de Provence or other blend of herbs
> 1 tsp extra-virgin Olive Oil

Add flavor ingredient (optional)... give a quick stir to combine.

> 1/2 cup (2-1/4 oz can) sliced Black Olives or 1/2 heaping tsp minced Garlic (jar) or other flavor ingredient of your choice

Add flour... stir until dough forms a shaggy ball, scrape dry flour from side of bowl, then tumble dough to combine moist flour with dry flour.

> 2 cups Bread Flour

Cover bowl with plastic wrap, place in a warm draft-free location, and proof for 1-1/2 hours.

1-1/2 hours later

When dough has risen and developed its gluten structure...

"Degas, pull and stretch"... stick handle end of a plastic spoon in the dough and stir (the dough will form a sticky ball). Then, scrape the side of the bowl to get the remainder of the dough into the sticky dough ball.

"Roll-to-coat"... sprinkle dough ball and side of bowl with flour and roll-to-coat (dusting dough ball with flour will make it easier to handle and shape dough).

> 2 Tbsp Bread Flour

Place a silicone baking mat on the work surface and roll dough (and excess flour) out of bowl onto mat.

Press lightly to flatten and shape into a medium size circle... cover with a lint-free towel, and rest for 10 minutes.

Congratulations, you have a fougasse dough ball.

Herb-Black Olive Fougasse

Prep: Move rack to the middle of oven and preheat to 450 degrees F.

Shape: Place a silicone baking mat on the work surface and roll dough (and excess flour) out of bowl onto mat.

<u>1 Fougasse Dough Ball with 1/2 cup sliced Black Olives</u>

Press lightly to flatten and shape into a medium size circle... cover with a lint-free towel and rest for 10 minutes.

After resting for 10 minutes... drizzle with olive oil, and use a pizza roller (or rolling pin) to spread the oil and form a small circle, turn dough over, drizzle 2nd side with oil, and use the roller to shape the dough into a leaf.

<u>1 tsp extra-virgin Olive Oil per side</u>

Use plastic bowl scraper to cut slits then stretch to open and spread.

Bake: Slide cookie sheet under silicone baking mat, place dough (cookie sheet and all) into the oven and bake for 15 minutes.

Serve: Remove from oven and serve with olive oil for dipping.

Notes: Fougasse (like all other flatbreads) doesn't need a 2nd proofing... it can be used immediately.

Garlic-Herb Fougasse

Prep: Move rack to the middle of oven and preheat to 450 degrees F.

Shape: Place a silicone baking mat on the work surface and roll dough (and excess flour) out of bowl onto mat.

<u>1 Fougasse Dough Ball with 1/2 heaping tsp minced Garlic (jar)</u>

Press lightly to flatten and shape into a medium size circle... cover with a lint-free towel and rest for 10 minutes.

After resting for 10 minutes... drizzle with olive oil, and use a pizza roller (or rolling pin) to spread the oil and form a small circle, turn dough over, drizzle 2nd side with oil, and use the roller to shape the dough into a leaf.

<u>1 tsp extra-virgin Olive Oil per side</u>

Use plastic bowl scraper to cut slits then stretch to open and spread.

Bake: Slide cookie sheet under silicone baking mat, place dough (cookie sheet and all) into the oven and bake for 15 minutes.

Serve: Remove from oven and serve with olive oil for dipping.

Notes: Fougasse (like all other flatbreads) doesn't need a 2nd proofing... it can be used immediately.

Restaurant Style Flatbread

Restaurant style flatbread has become very popular in upscale restaurants. The key is the thin crust which makes it light and versatile... ideal for an appetizer.

I have three restaurant style dough recipes to fit your lifestyle and taste...

    (a) "Turbo" no-knead flatbread dough: Light airy crust.

    (b) Yogurt enhanced flatbread dough: Soft medium crust.

    (c) No-yeast flatbread dough: Very thin crust.

...and three methods which allow baked and/or fresh ingredients.

    (a) Traditional pizza style: Roll flatbread very thin, add toppings and bake flatbread and toppings together.

    (b) Fresh toppings: Roll flatbread very thin, bake flatbread, then add fresh toppings (ideal for fresh strawberries or mixed greens).

    (c) Warmed fresh toppings: Roll flatbread very thin, bake flatbread, add fresh toppings, then heat flatbread with toppings (ideal for blueberries).

The options are up to you... baked toppings... fresh toppings... or warm fresh toppings.

"For the first time ever,
overweight people outnumber average people in America.
Doesn't that make overweight the average then?
Last month you were fat, now you're average - hey, let's get a pizza!"

Jay Leno, *The Tonight Show*

Restaurant Style "Turbo" No-Knead Flatbread Dough

Some restaurants use traditional pizza dough with a little extra olive oil... the olive oil conditions the dough making it easier to roll a thin flatbread.

Pour warm water in a 3 to 3-1/2 qt warm glass mixing bowl (use a warm bowl... you don't want a cold bowl to take the heat out of the warm water).

> 6 oz warm Water

Add salt, yeast, and olive oil... give a quick stir to combine.

> 1 tsp Salt
> 1 tsp Instant Yeast
> 1 Tbsp extra-virgin Olive Oil

Add flour... stir until dough forms a shaggy ball, scrape dry flour from side of bowl, then tumble dough to combine moist flour with dry flour.

> 1-1/2 cups Bread Flour

Cover bowl with plastic wrap, place in a warm draft-free location, and proof for 1-1/2 hours.

1-1/2 hours later

When dough has risen and developed its gluten structure...

"Degas, pull and stretch"... stick handle end of a plastic spoon in the dough and stir (the dough will form a sticky ball). Then, scrape the side of the bowl to get the remainder of the dough into the sticky dough ball.

"Roll-to-coat"... sprinkle dough ball and side of bowl with flour and roll-to-coat (dusting dough ball with flour will make it easier to handle and shape dough).

> 2 Tbsp Bread Flour

Dust work surface with flour, roll dough (and excess flour) out of bowl onto work surface.

Press lightly to flatten, divide into 2 portions and form each portion into an elongated disc, then use a pizza roller to flatten and spread into an oval (9" x 12") or long strip (7" x 18") 1/8" thick, dusting with flour as needed.

Option:

Traditional – Use 1/4 tsp instant Yeast and "Traditional Method" (proof over night).

Restaurant Style "Yogurt" Flatbread Dough

This recipe uses yogurt as its wet ingredient. The dough can be rolled very thin and the yogurt gives the flatbread a soft texture.

Add flour to a 3 to 3-1/2 qt glass mixing bowl.

> 1-1/2 cups Self-Rising Flour

or (make your own self-rising flour)...

> 1-1/2 cups All-Purpose Flour
> 1-1/2 tsp Baking Powder
> 3/4 tsp Salt
> 1/2 tsp Baking Soda

Add yogurt and water... start by stirring with the handle end of a plastic spoon (I like to use a flat whisk to slice through yogurt), then use a spatula to scrape the side of the bowl a little at a time and press the dry ingredients into the wet until combined.

> 1 container (6 oz) Greek Yogurt
> 2 oz Water

Roll dough (and excess flour) out of bowl onto work surface and knead for 1 minute to fully combine ingredients.

Cover with a lint-free towel, and rest for 30 minutes.

30 minutes later

After dough has rested... generously dust work surface with flour, press lightly to flatten, divide into 2 portions and form each portion into an elongated disc, then use a pizza roller to flatten and spread into an oval (9" x 12") or long strip (7" x 18") 1/8" thick, dusting with flour as needed.

Restaurant Style "No Yeast" Flatbread Dough

Flatbread does not require a leavening agent... it's flat.

Pour water in a 3 to 3-1/2 qt glass mixing bowl.

<u>6 oz Water</u>

Add salt and olive oil... give a quick stir to combine.

<u>1 tsp Salt</u>

<u>3 Tbsp extra-virgin Olive Oil</u>

Add flour... stir with the handle end of a plastic spoon to mix moisture into flour, then use a spatula to scrape the side of the bowl and press the dry ingredients into the wet until fully combined.

<u>2 cups All-Purpose Flour</u>

Roll dough (and excess flour) out of bowl onto work surface and knead for 1 minute to fully combine ingredients.

Cover with a lint-free towel, and rest for 30 minutes.

30 minutes later

After dough has rested... generously dust work surface with flour, press lightly to flatten, divide into 2 portions and form each portion into an elongated disc, then use a pizza roller to flatten and spread into an oval (9" x 12") or long strip (7" x 18") 1/8" thick, dusting with flour as needed.

Classic Cheese Flatbread

Sometimes the simplest is the most popular.

Prep: Move rack to the middle of oven, preheat to 450 degrees F, and place flatbread on bakeware (cookie sheet, rimmed baking pan, silicone baking mat, etc.) prior to adding toppings so that it can be moved to the oven without disturbing its shape or toppings.

     Flatbread

Toppings: Spread a thin layer of sauce on flatbread, sprinkle with cheese.

     2 heaping Tbsp Pizza Sauce

     4 oz shredded Provolone & Mozzarella Cheese

Bake: Slide flatbread into oven and bake for 10 to 12 minutes at 450 degrees F.

Serve: Remove from oven and serve.

Pesto-Black Olive Flatbread

This is a very popular appetizer flatbread that is very easy to make.

Prep: Move rack to the middle of oven, preheat to 450 degrees F, and place flatbread on bakeware (cookie sheet, rimmed baking pan, silicone baking mat, etc.) prior to adding toppings so that it can be moved to the oven without disturbing its shape or toppings.

<u>Flatbread</u>

Toppings: Add garlic paste and spread with kitchen knife, add pesto and spread with back of spoon, and cover with olives.

<u>2 tsp Garlic Paste</u>
<u>2 heaping Tbsp Pesto</u>
<u>1/2 cup (2-1/4 oz can) sliced Black Olives</u>

Bake: Slide flatbread into oven and bake for 10 to 12 minutes at 450 degrees F.

Serve: Remove from oven and serve.

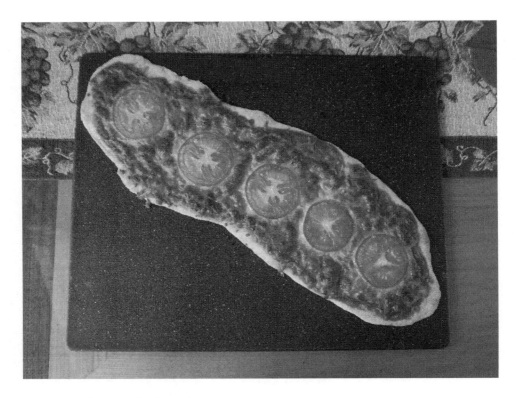

Tomato-Cheese Flatbread

Prep: Move rack to the middle of oven, preheat to 450 degrees F, and place flatbread on bakeware (cookie sheet, rimmed baking pan, silicone baking mat, etc.) prior to adding toppings so that it can be moved to the oven without disturbing its shape or toppings.

      Flatbread

Toppings: Spread a thin layer of sauce on flatbread, sprinkle with cheese, and add tomato slices.

      2 heaping Tbsp Pizza Sauce

      4 oz shredded Provolone & Mozzarella Cheese

      5 thin Tomato slices

Bake: Slide flatbread into oven and bake for 10 to 12 minutes at 450 degrees F.

Serve: Remove from oven and serve.

Pepperoni-Bacon Flatbread

Prep: Move rack to the middle of oven, preheat to 450 degrees F, and place flatbread on bakeware (cookie sheet, rimmed baking pan, silicone baking mat, etc.) prior to adding toppings so that it can be moved to the oven without disturbing its shape or toppings.

Flatbread

Toppings: Spread a thin layer of sauce on flatbread, sprinkle with cheese, add pepperoni to cover 75%, add bacon between pepperoni slices, add black olives for color, and sprinkle with a little more cheese.

2 heaping Tbsp Pizza Sauce
4 oz shredded Provolone & Mozzarella Cheese
Sliced Pepperoni
3 slices precooked Bacon cut into 1/2" bites
2 oz sliced Black Olives

Bake: Slide flatbread into oven and bake for 10 to 12 minutes at 450 degrees F.
Serve: Remove from oven and serve.

Bacon, Bacon, Bacon Flatbread

If you love bacon, you'll love this flatbread.

Prep: Move rack to the middle of oven, preheat to 450 degrees F, and place flatbread on bakeware (cookie sheet, rimmed baking pan, silicone baking mat, etc.) prior to adding toppings so that it can be moved to the oven without disturbing its shape or toppings.

      Flatbread

Toppings: Spread a thin layer of sauce on flatbread, sprinkle with cheese, and add bacon.

      2 heaping Tbsp Pizza Sauce

      4 oz shredded Provolone & Mozzarella Cheese

      5 slices precooked Bacon cut in half

Bake: Slide flatbread into oven and bake for 10 to 12 minutes at 450 degrees F.

Serve: Remove from oven and serve.

Mexican Jalapeño-Chili Fiesta Flatbread

Prep: Move rack to the middle of oven, preheat to 450 degrees F, and place flatbread on bakeware (cookie sheet, rimmed baking pan, silicone baking mat, etc.) prior to adding toppings so that it can be moved to the oven without disturbing its shape or toppings.

    Flatbread

Toppings: Sprinkle with cheese, add chilies and green peppers to cover, add roasted red pepper and corn for color.

    4 oz shredded Pepper Jack or Provolone-Mozzarella Cheese
    2 whole Green Chilies (sliced lengthwise)
    Fresh Jalapeño Peppers slices
    Roasted Red Peppers
    Golden Sweet Corn

Bake: Slide flatbread into oven and bake for 10 to 12 minutes at 450 degrees F.
Serve: Remove from oven and serve.

Asparagus Flatbread

Prep: Move rack to the middle of oven, preheat to 450 degrees F, and place flatbread on bakeware (cookie sheet, rimmed baking pan, silicone baking mat, etc.) prior to adding toppings so that it can be moved to the oven without disturbing its shape or toppings.

       Flatbread

Toppings: Drizzle with oil and spread, add minced garlic and spread, sprinkle with cheese, add asparagus and garnish with parmesan cheese and lemon slices.

       1 Tbsp Vegetable Oil
       1 Tbsp Minced Garlic
       2 oz Italian Cheese Blend
       Asparagus
       1 oz Parmesan Cheese
       2 Lemon slices

Bake: Slide flatbread into oven and bake for 10 to 12 minutes at 450 degrees F.

Serve: Remove from oven and serve.

Fresh Strawberry Flatbread

This is a good example of baking the flatbread... then adding fresh toppings.

Prep: Move rack to the middle of oven, preheat to 450 degrees F, and place flatbread on bakeware (cookie sheet, rimmed baking pan, silicone baking mat, etc.) prior to adding toppings so that it can be moved to the oven without disturbing its shape or toppings.

    Flatbread

Drizzle with olive oil and spread oil with pizza roller.

    1 tsp extra-virgin Olive Oil

Bake: Slide flatbread into oven and bake for 10 to 12 minutes at 450 degrees F.

Meanwhile...

Prep: Combine ricotta cheese, olive oil, sugar, salt, and dried basil... and set aside.

    8 oz Ricotta Cheese
    2 tsp extra-virgin Olive Oil
    2 tsp Sugar
    1/4 tsp Salt
    1/2 tsp dried Basil

12 minutes later...

Top & Serve: Remove from oven... spread ricotta cheese mixture on flatbread with a small spatula, add strawberries, garnish with fresh basil, and serve.

    Strawberries
    Fresh Basil

Fresh Blueberry-Basil Flatbread
This is a good example of baking the flatbread... adding fresh toppings... and heating the flatbread and toppings.

Prep: Move rack to the middle of oven, preheat to 450 degrees F, and place flatbread on bakeware (cookie sheet, rimmed baking pan, silicone baking mat, etc.) prior to adding toppings so that it can be moved to the oven without disturbing its shape or toppings.
       Flatbread
Drizzle with olive oil and spread oil with pizza roller.
       1 tsp extra-virgin Olive Oil
Bake: Slide flatbread into oven and bake for 10 to 12 minutes at 450 degrees F.

Meanwhile...
Prep: Combine ricotta cheese, olive oil, salt, and dried basil... and set aside.
       8 oz Ricotta Cheese
       2 tsp extra-virgin Olive Oil
       1/4 tsp Salt
       1/2 tsp dried Basil

12 minutes later...
Fresh Toppings: Remove from oven... spread ricotta cheese mixture on flatbread with a small spatula and add blueberries.
       Fresh Blueberries
Heat: Put back in the oven to heat for 3 minutes.
Garnish & Serve: Remove from oven, garnish with fresh basil, and serve.
       Fresh Basil

Restaurant Style Pan Grilled Flatbread with Trio

Prep: Place silicone baking mat on work space and put a 12" non-stick skillet on cooktop, turn to med-high, and drizzle with oil.

<u>1 tsp Vegetable Oil</u>

Shape: Lightly dust work surface and dough with flour, press to flatten, divide each dough ball into 4 portions and set 3 aside.

<u>2 Restaurant Style Yogurt Flatbread Dough Balls</u>

Then (one portion at a time)... press lightly to flatten, drizzle with oil and spread oil with pizza roller. Then, turn dough over, drizzle 2nd side with oil, and roll into a 7 to 8" circle 1/8" thick.

<u>1 tsp Vegetable Oil per side</u>

Pan Grill: Grill 1 minute, flip and grill 30 second.

While grilling... prepare next portion.

Serve: Remove from skillet, slice into 8 wedges, and serve warm.

Note: We like to add 1 teaspoon ground coriander when making this dough.

Hummus, Pesto, Olive Tapenade Trio

Flatbread is the pallet... the potato chip... for delivering a variety of toppings and the hummus, pesto hummus and olive tapenade will make it the perfect appetizer.

Hummus

Sabra Roasted Pine Nut Hummus

Pesto Hummus

1 part pesto
6 parts hummus

Olive Tapenade

Combine ingredients in a food processor.

1/2 cup (2-1/4 oz can) sliced Black Olives
1/2 cup stuffed Green Olives
1/2 cup pitted Kalamata Olives
Zest of 1 Lemon
1 heaping tsp Capers
1 heaping tsp Minced Garlic
1/4 cup fresh Parsley Leaves

Pulse several times until coarsely chopped and well blended.
Continue to pulse, slowly adding olive oil.

2 to 3 oz extra-virgin Olive Oil

Serve

Place pre-made hummus and the tapenade in separate serving bowls.
Slice flatbread rounds into 8 wedges.
On a long serving platter... place spreads in middle, surround the spreads with flatbread, and put a small knife on each end of the platter.
Garnish with berries and herbs.

Notes: At times we substitute Avocado Hummus for the Pesto Hummus which is 1 part Avocado with 1 part *Sabra* Roasted Pine Nut Hummus.

Basic Flatbread

Before our ancient ancestors discovered yeast or kneading they made flatbreads with flour, water and salt… and many cultures have linked traditions to the flatbreads of their ancestors. There are a wide variety of flatbreads… tortilla, pita, nana, focaccia, pizza, etc. Some have leavening agents (yeast, baking soda, baking powder, etc.) and some don't.

Basic Pan Grilled Flatbread

Pour warm water in a 3 to 4 qt warm glass mixing bowl (use a warm bowl... you don't want a cold bowl to take the heat out of the warm water).

<u>14 oz Water</u>

Add salt, yeast, and olive oil... give a quick stir to combine.

<u>1-1/2 tsp Salt</u>
<u>1-1/4 tsp Instant Yeast</u>
<u>1 Tbsp extra-virgin Olive Oil</u>

Add flour... stir until dough forms a shaggy ball, scrape dry flour from side of bowl, then tumble dough to combine moist flour with dry flour.

<u>3-1/2 cups Bread Flour</u>

Cover bowl with plastic wrap, place in a warm draft-free location, and proof for 1-1/2 hours.

1-1/2 hours later

When dough has risen and developed its gluten structure...

"Degas, pull and stretch"... stick handle end of a plastic spoon in the dough and stir (the dough will form a sticky ball). Then, scrape the side of the bowl to get the remainder of the dough into the sticky dough ball.

"Roll-to-coat"... sprinkle dough ball and side of bowl with flour and roll-to-coat (dusting dough ball with flour will make it easier to handle and shape dough).

<u>2 Tbsp Bread Flour</u>

Dust work surface with flour, roll dough (and excess flour) out of bowl onto work surface.

Press lightly to flatten… divide dough into 4 portions (like a pizza) and form each portion into a ball (add flour as needed to assist with shaping), and set aside.

Pan grilled

Place 12" non-stick skillet on cooktop, turn to med-high, and drizzle with a little olive oil.

Then (one portion at a time)… press lightly to flatten, drizzle with oil and spread oil with pizza roller , turn dough over, drizzle 2nd side with oil, and shape with roller into a circle 1/8" to 1/4" thick.

    1 tsp extra-virgin Olive Oil

Add a dab of garlic paste (or garlic salt, etc.), and spread with roller.

    1 tsp Garlic Paste

Place dough in skillet and grill for about 3 minutes per side.

Remove from skillet and serve warm.

30211705R00042

Printed in Great Britain
by Amazon